SAINT

聖パウロ200語

WITH JAPANESE TRANSLATION

Compiled by
Stean Anthony

Yamaguchi Shoten, Kyoto

山口書店, 京都

Greek words on the cover
Romans 1.1
Illustration of Saint Paul
© 2009 Stean Anthony

Hear my voice at:
http://www35.tok2.com/home/stean2/

Saint Paul 200
© 2010 Stean Anthony
Author's profits for Oxfam Japan,
see end of book for details
PRINTED IN JAPAN

FOR ALL WHO LOVE GOD

Preface

This book is an anthology of phrases and sentences taken from the Letters of Saint Paul. It is part of my MTMM series – a dialogue between faiths for better understanding and peace. In particular, the series began with a prayer for greater trust and understanding between Islam and the Church, and I have made this anthology with that purpose in mind.

I therefore chose phrases that illustrate Saint Paul's wisdom, and which are also easy to share. My comments add an extra perspective. It's my version of what a modern Paul might be, building bridges for love.

If you have no faith in God, you may read the word God as meaning "the greatest goodness" – which can be found in the hearts and minds of all.

In general, traditional order is followed: Acts, Romans, Corinthians, Galatians, Ephesians, Philippians, Colossians, Thessalonians, Timothy, Titus and Philemon.

序文

この本は聖パウロの手紙から引用された格言・金言の選集です。そして私の『母へのメッセージ』のシリーズの、より良い相互理解と平和のための信仰間の対話の一巻でもあります。とりわけこのシリーズは、イスラム教とキリスト教会の間のより大きな信頼と理解のための祈りから始まっており、私はその目的を心に願いながらこの選集を作りました。

それゆえ聖パウロの叡智を表し、なおかつ分かち合いやすい格言を選びました。私のコメントはさらなる展望を与えるでしょう。それは愛の橋渡しをするために、聖パウロが現代にいたならば、かくあるだろうという私の解釈です。

もし、あなたが神への信仰を持っていなければ、「神」という言葉を、生きとし生ける全てのものの心にみられる「最大の善良さ」という意味で読んでください。

一般的に、聖パウロのことばの伝統的な順番は次のようになっています。

使徒言行録、ローマ、コリント、ガラテヤ、エフェソ、フィリピ、コロサイ、テサロニケ、テモテ、テトス、フィレモン、の順番です。

序文翻訳:林智之

One

Rejoice in hope, be patient in suffering, persevere in prayer.
Rom 12.12

Comment
Hold nothing back from God when you pray.

***

Two

Love one another with mutual affection.
Rom 12.10

Comment
Let the broken world mend.

Three

Then he knelt down and cried out in a loud voice, "Lord, do not hold this sin against them." When he had said this, he died. And Saul approved of their killing him.
Acts 7.60 – 8.1

Comment
Saul is Paul.

***

Four

That day a severe persecution began.
Acts 8.1

Comment
Get through somehow.

Five

Both men and women, he committed them to prison.
Acts 8.3

Comment
He imprisons himself.

***

Six

Now as he was going along and approaching Damascus, suddenly a light from heaven flashed around him. He fell to the ground and heard a voice saying to him, "Saul, Saul, why do you persecute me?" He asked, "Who are you, Lord?"
Acts 9.3-5

Comment
For three days he was without sight, and neither ate nor drank c. 35 CE.

Seven

About noon a great light from heaven.
Acts 22.6

Comment
Love more.

***

Eight

The men who were traveling with him stood speechless, because they heard the voice, but saw no one.
Acts 9.7

Comment
You will know what you have to do.

Nine

What am I to do, Lord?
Acts 22.10

Comment
Give them this word – Freedom!

***

Ten

Now, why do you delay?
Acts 22.16

Comment
Make love real.

Eleven

Something like scales fell from his eyes, and his sight was restored.
Acts 9.18

Comment
Tears of sorrow and joy.

***

Twelve

Go, for I will send you far away.
Acts 22.21

Comment
Speaking to women now.

Thirteen

Barnabus went to Tarsus to look for Saul, and when he had found him, he brought him to Antioch.
Acts 11.25-6

Comment
Ancient walls, new prayers.

***

Fourteen

Paul, filled with the Holy Spirit, looked intently at him.
Acts 13.9

Comment
Build love.

Fifteen

Descendants of Abraham's family, and others who fear God, to us the message of this salvation has been sent.
Acts 13.26

Comment
Love one another better, can this message be heard by all of us, in a prayer for peace?

***

Sixteen

Paul, looking at him intently and seeing that he had faith to be healed, said in a loud voice, "Stand upright on your feet." And the man sprang up and began to walk.
Acts 14.9-10

Comment
Healing others he heals himself.

Seventeen

Am I trying to please people?
Gal 1.10

Comment
Please and displease.

***

Eighteen

It is a very small thing that I should be judged by you or by any human court.
1 Cor 4.3

Comment
Be confident like Paul.

Nineteen

What would you prefer? Am I to come to you with a stick?
1 Cor 4.21

Comment
More kindness, please.

***

Twenty

In Damascus, the governor under King Aretas guarded the city of Damascus in order to seize me, but I was let down in a basket through a window in the wall, and escaped from his hands.
2 Cor 11.32

Comment
Freedom to those who love God.

Twenty-One

I know a person in Christ who fourteen years ago was caught up to the third heaven – whether in the body or out of the body I do not know, God knows. And I know that such a person ... was caught up into Paradise and heard things that are not to be told, that no mortal is permitted to repeat.
2 Cor 12.2

Comment
This was Paul.

***

Twenty-Two

A thorn was given me in the flesh.
2 Cor 12.7

Comment
When I'm weak, I'm strong.

Twenty-Three

I, Paul, write this greeting with my own hand.
2 Thess 3.17

Comment
Don't you recognize me?

***

Twenty-Four

I have become all things to all people, that I might by all means save some.
1 Cor 9.22

Comment
Love does not alter.

Twenty-Five

What persecutions I endured!
2 Tim 3.11

Comment
Imprisoned, beaten, scorned.

***

Twenty-Six

On the sabbath day we went outside the gate by the river, where we supposed there was a place of prayer; and we sat down and spoke to the women who had gathered there. A certain woman named Lydia, a worshiper of God, was listening to us; she was from the city of Thyatira and a dealer in purple cloth.
Acts 16.13-14

Comment
The Lord opened her heart to listen eagerly to what was said by Paul.

Twenty-Seven

One day, as we were going to the place of prayer, we met a slave-girl who had a spirit of divination and brought her owners a great deal of money by fortune-telling. While she followed Paul and us, she would cry out.
Acts 16.16-17

Comment
These men are slaves of the Most High God, who proclaim to you a way of salvation.

***

Twenty-Eight

They have beaten us in public, uncondemned, men who are Roman citizens, and have thrown us into prison; and now are they going to discharge us in secret? Certainly not! Let them come and take us out themselves.
Acts 16.37

Comment
Too stubborn for his own good.

Twenty-Nine

These people who have been turning the world upside down have come here also.
Acts 17.6

Comment
Lift up the poor, cast down the mighty.

***

Thirty

I found among them an altar with the inscription, "To an unknown god." What therefore you worship as unknown, this I proclaim to you.
Acts 17.23

Comment
Paul in Athens, Areopagus.

Thirty-One

For "In Him we live and move and have our being"; as even some of your own poets have said, "For we too are His offspring."
Acts 17.28

Comment
Paul quotes ancient Greeks.

***

Thirty-Two

Risked their necks for my life.
Rom 16.4

Comment
Prisca and Aquila. Acts 18.2. 1 Cor 16.19.

Thirty-Three

Great is Artemis of the Ephesians!
Acts 19.28

Comment
Temple of Diana, a wonder of the world.

***

Thirty-Four

It is more blessed to give than to receive.
Acts 20.35

Comment
Blessed are the merciful.

Thirty-Five

When he had finished speaking, he knelt down with them all and prayed. There was much weeping among them all; they embraced Paul and kissed him, grieving especially because of what he had said, that they would not see him again.
Acts 20.36-38

Comment
They loved him.

***

Thirty-Six

Paul replied, "I am a Jew, from Tarsus in Cilicia, a citizen."
Acts 21.39

Comment
I demand freedom for my friends.

Thirty-Seven

We find nothing wrong with this man. What if a spirit or an angel has spoken to him?
Acts 23.9

Comment
Be slow to condemn.

***

Thirty-Eight

That night the Lord stood near him and said, "Keep up your courage!"
Acts 23.11

Comment
Stand by all prisoners.

Thirty-Nine

To open their eyes so that they may turn from darkness to light.
Acts 26.18

Comment
Appointed to serve God.

***

Forty

He took bread; and giving thanks to God in the presence of all, he broke it.
Acts 27.35

Comment
All were brought safely to land.

Forty-One

Cured him by praying and putting his hands on him.
Acts 28.8

Comment
All be healed.

***

Forty-Two

We would like to hear from you what you think, for with regard to this sect we know that everywhere it is spoken against.
Acts 28.22

Comment
Sign of truth.

Forty-Three

For I am longing to see you so that I may share with you some spiritual gift to strengthen you – or rather so that we may be mutually encouraged by each other's faith, both yours and mine.
Rom 1.11-12

Comment
Leap the barrier of faith.

***

Forty-Four

It is written, "The one who is righteous will live by faith."
Rom 1.17

Comment
Read the old books.

Forty-Five

For those who are self-seeking and who obey not the truth but wickedness, there will be wrath and fury.
Rom 2.8

Comment
Glory, honor and peace for those who do good.

***

Forty-Six

Is God the God of Jews only?
Rom 3.29

Comment
God beyond time.

Forty-Seven

For what does the scripture say? "Abraham believed God, and it was reckoned to him as righteousness."
Rom 4.3

Comment
Stronger faith lifts higher.

***

Forty-Eight

Suffering produces endurance, and endurance produces character, and character produces hope.
Rom 5.3-4

Comment
Lessen the suffering of others.

Forty-Nine

For the wages of sin is death.
Rom 6.23

Comment
What is sin?

***

Fifty

New life of the Spirit.
Rom 7.6

Comment
Love better, forget the rest.

Fifty-One

I do not do the good I want.
Rom 7.19

Comment
Peace in Jerusalem.

***

Fifty-Two

If God is for us, who is against us?
Rom 8.31

Comment
Soul, shine with goodness.

Fifty-Three

Will what is molded say to the one who molds it, "Why have you made me like this?"
Rom 9.20

Comment
Born with a flaw.

***

Fifty-Four

As it is written, "How beautiful are the feet of those who bring good news!"
Rom 10.16

Comment
"How welcome are they who proclaim peace!" Isaiah 52.7.

Fifty-Five

Faith comes from what is heard.
Rom 10.17

Comment
Listen to heaven.

***

Fifty-Six

You, a wild olive shoot, were grafted.
Rom 11.17

Comment
Serve one another in love.

Fifty-Seven

O the depth of the riches and wisdom
And knowledge of God!
Rom 11.33

Comment
Sing!

***

Fifty-Eight

Let love be genuine; hate what is evil, hold fast to what is good.
Rom 12.9

Comment
Agree with your neighbor.

Fifty-Nine

Contribute to the needs of the saints. Extend hospitality to strangers.
Rom 12.13

Comment
Learn from saints and strangers.

***

Sixty

Bless those who persecute you; bless and do not curse them.
Rom 12.14

Comment
Respond with goodness.

Sixty-One

Live in harmony with one another.
Rom 12.16

Comment
All life on earth.

***

Sixty-Two

Associate with the lowly.
Rom 12.16

Comment
Give better life.

Sixty-Three

Never avenge yourselves.
Rom 12.19

Comment
Give love.

***

Sixty-Four

If your enemies are hungry, feed them; if they are thirsty, give them something to drink.
Rom 12.20

Comment
Make them friends.

Sixty-Five

Let every person be subject to the governing authorities; for there is no authority except from God, and those authorities that exist have been instituted by God.
Rom 13.1

Comment
Not Caesar! Go underground.

***

Sixty-Six

Love your neighbor as yourself.
Rom 13.9

Comment
All are neighbors.

Sixty-Seven

Love does no wrong to a neighbor; therefore, love is the fulfilling of the law.
Rom 13.10

Comment
Love one another with a gentle heart.

***

Sixty-Eight

It is now the moment for you to wake.
Rom 13.11

Comment
With the dawn.

Sixty-Nine

The night is far gone, the day is near.
Rom 13.12

Comment
Hope rising.

***

Seventy

Put on the armor of light.
Rom 13.12

Comment
God is love.

Seventy-One

Some judge one day to be better than another, while others judge all days to be alike.
Rom 14.5

Comment
This day is holy.

***

Seventy-Two

I commend to you our sister Phoebe, a deacon of the church at Cenchreae, so that you may welcome her.
Rom 16.1

Comment
Welcome her.

Seventy-Three

God is faithful.
1 Cor 1.9

Comment
Paul liked this.

***

Seventy-Four
All of you be in agreement and that there be no divisions among you – but that you be united in the same mind and the same purpose.
1 Cor 1.10

Comment
To seize the future.

Seventy-Five

Has not God made foolish the wisdom of the world?
1 Cor 1.20

Comment
True love is folly.

***

Seventy-Six

God chose what is weak in the world to shame the strong.
1 Cor 1.27

Comment
When I'm strong, I'm weak.

Seventy-Seven

No eye has seen, nor ear heard, nor the human heart conceived.
1 Cor 2.9

Comment
Hidden truth of surpassing glory.

***

Seventy-Eight

Taught by the Spirit, interpreting spiritual things.
1 Cor 2.13

Comment
Wind through the soul.

Seventy-Nine

As long as there is jealousy and quarreling among you, are you not of the flesh?
1 Cor 3.3

Comment
People of spirit meet in kindness.

***

Eighty

God's temple is holy and you are that temple.
1 Cor 3.17

Comment
All life on earth.

Eighty-One

Do not pronounce judgment before the time.
1 Cor 4.5

Comment
Innocent of harm, I say good.

***

Eighty-Two

When reviled, we bless; when persecuted, we endure;
when slandered, we speak kindly.
1 Cor 4.12-13

Comment
This is best.

Eighty-Three

The rubbish of the world.
1 Cor 4.13

Comment
Pick up litter everywhere.

***

Eighty-Four

With love in a spirit of gentleness.
1 Cor 4.21

Comment
Clean the world.

Eighty-Five

You were washed, you were sanctified.
1 Cor 6.11

Comment
Hate became love.

***

Eighty-Six

The present form of the world is passing.
1 Cor 7.31

Comment
The world is always ending.

Eighty-Seven

What then is my reward?
1 Cor 9.18

Comment
To be loved, and to love.

***

Eighty-Eight

Do you not know that in a race the runners all compete, but only one receives the prize?
1 Cor 9.24

Comment
All get prizes.

Eighty-Nine

Run in such a way that you may win it.
1 Cor 9.24

Comment
Win the best.

***

Ninety

Exercise self-control in all things.
1 Cor 9.25

Comment
Do not give suffering to others.

Ninety-One

God is faithful, and he will not let you be tested beyond your strength, but with the testing he will also provide the way out so that you may be able to endure it.
1 Cor 10.13

Comment
Door open to let love in.

***

Ninety-Two

Flee from the worship of idols.
1 Cor 10.14

Comment
Anger and hate – these are idols.

Ninety-Three

Because there is one bread, we who are many are one body, for we all partake of the one bread.
1 Cor 10.17

Comment
Break the bread of peace together.

***

Ninety-Four

Judge for yourselves, is it proper?
1 Cor 11.13

Comment
A woman to pray to God with her head unveiled?

Ninety-Five

Do this in remembrance of me.
1 Cor 11.24-25

Comment
Remember how you are loved.

***

Ninety-Six

There are varieties.
1 Cor 12.4-6

Comment
Only love is real.

Ninety-Seven

To one is given through the Spirit the utterance of wisdom, and to another the utterance of knowledge according to the same Spirit, to another faith by the same Spirit, to another gifts of healing.
1 Cor 12.8-10

Comment
Each has something to give.

***

Ninety-Eight

As it is, there are many members, yet one body.
1 Cor 12.20

Comment
Gather us all together again.

Ninety-Nine

If I speak in the tongues of mortals and of angels, but do not have love, I am a noisy gong or a clanging cymbal.
1 Cor 13.1

Comment
Chiming – peace be in your house.

***

One Hundred

If I have prophetic powers, and understand all mysteries and all knowledge, and if I have all faith, so as to remove mountains, but do not have love, I am nothing.
1 Cor 13.2

Comment
Find God in this truth.

One Hundred One

If I give away all my possessions, and if I hand over my body so that I may boast, but do not have love, I gain nothing.
1 Cor 13.3

Comment
How can we thank you?

***

One Hundred Two

If I give away all my possessions, and if I hand over my body to be burned, but do not have love, I gain nothing.
1 Cor. 13.3

Comment
Greater love had no one.

Manuscripts vary in this verse

One Hundred Three

Love is patient. Love is kind.
1 Cor 13.4

Comment
Find love and follow.

***

One Hundred Four

Love bears all things, believes all things, hopes all things, endures all things.
1 Cor 13.7

Comment
Beyond self a mystical surrender.

One Hundred Five

Love never ends.
1 Cor 13.8

Comment
Believe this.

***

One Hundred Six

For we know only in part.
1 Cor 13.9

Comment
One day, all will be perfect.

One Hundred Seven

For now we see in a mirror, dimly, but then we will see face to face.
1 Cor 13.12

Comment
Enigma of God's love.

***

One Hundred Eight

Now I know only in part; then I will know fully, even as I have been fully known.
1 Cor 13.12

Comment
All is partial, perfect beyond.

One Hundred Nine

Faith, hope and love abide, these three; and the greatest of these is love.
1 Cor 13.13

Comment
When doctrine says "I will not love," then cast it away.

***

One Hundred Ten

Pursue love.
1 Cor. 14.1

Comment
Greek *agape*, Latin *caritas*, Japanese ai 愛.

互いに愛し合いなさい。

One Hundred Eleven

Instruments that produce sound, such as the flute or the harp.
1 Cor 14.7

Comment
Sweet melody in the heart.

***

One Hundred Twelve

Women should be silent in the churches.
1 Cor 14.34

Comment
Speak. Do not be silent.

One Hundred Thirteen

Last of all, as to one untimely born, he appeared also to me. For I am the least of the apostles, unfit to be called an apostle, because I persecuted.
1 Cor 15.8-9

Comment
His grace to Paul was not in vain.

***

One Hundred Fourteen

I worked harder than any of them – though it was not I, but the grace of God.
1 Cor 15.10

Comment
Is he boasting?

One Hundred Fifteen

When I arrive, I will send any whom you approve with letters to take your gift to Jerusalem.
1 Cor 16.3

Comment
Gifts of peace between us – all faiths.

***

One Hundred Sixteen

Keep alert, stand firm in your faith, be courageous, be strong. Let all that you do be done in love.
1 Cor 16.13-14

Comment
Tear down the fences to love.

One Hundred Seventeen

Greet one another with a holy kiss.
1 Cor 16.20

Comment
Touch hands in gentleness.

***

One Hundred Eighteen

Marana tha or Maran atha!
1 Cor 16.22

Comment
Love, shine brighter in my heart.

One Hundred Nineteen

We are workers with you for your joy.
2 Cor 1.24

Comment
Each to each, love's purpose.

***

One Hundred Twenty

Forgive and console.
2 Cor 2.7

Comment
Reaffirm your love.

One Hundred Twenty-One

Fragrance from life to life.
2 Cor 2.16

Comment
Air from heaven.

***

One Hundred Twenty-Two

The Spirit gives life.
2 Cor 3.6

Comment
Spirit teach us to love!

One Hundred Twenty-Three

The veil is removed.
2 Cor 3.16

Comment
Love seen in surpassing brightness.

***

One Hundred Twenty-Four

It is the God who said, "Let light shine out of darkness," who has shone in our hearts.
2 Cor 4.6

Comment
Lamp lit with holy oil.

One Hundred Twenty-Five

Treasure in clay jars.
2 Cor 4.7

Comment
Word of God within us.

***

One Hundred Twenty-Six

Afflicted in every way, but not crushed.
2 Cor 4.8

Comment
Suffer to love, if need be.

One Hundred Twenty-Seven

Even though our outer nature is wasting away, our inner nature is being renewed day by day.
2 Cor 4.16

Comment
Brighter spirit within.

***

One Hundred Twenty-Eight

We look not at what can be seen but at what cannot be seen; for what can be seen is temporary, but what cannot be seen is eternal.
2 Cor 4.18

Comment
Beyond illusion.

One Hundred Twenty-Nine

Everything old has passed away; see, everything has become new!
2 Cor 5.17

Comment
New every day.

***

One Hundred Thirty

We are treated as impostors, and yet are true, as unknown, and yet are well known.
2 Cor 6.8-9

Comment
Same truth, new clothes.

One Hundred Thirty-One

Open wide your hearts.
2 Cor 6.13

Comment
Rainbow over Africa.

***

One Hundred Thirty-Two

Make room in your hearts for us.
2 Cor 7.2

Comment
Child born to sorrow.

One Hundred Thirty-Three

The one who sows sparingly will also reap sparingly, and the one who sows bountifully will also reap bountifully.
2 Cor 9.6

Comment
Be active in goodness.

***

One Hundred Thirty-Four

God loves a cheerful giver.
2 Cor 9.7

Comment
Give every day.

One Hundred Thirty-Five

He scatters abroad, he gives to the poor.
2 Cor 9.9 & Ps 112.9

Comment
Lift Africa.

***

One Hundred Thirty-Six

For they say, "His letters are weighty and strong, but his bodily presence is weak, and his speech contemptible."
2 Cor 10.10

Comment
About Paul, by Paul – is the opposite true?

One Hundred Thirty-Seven

Because I do not love you? God knows I do!
2 Cor 11.11

Comment
So let them know this, then!

***

One Hundred Thirty-Eight

Even Satan disguises himself as an angel of light.
2 Cor 11.14

Comment
Hatred and selfishness is Satan.

One Hundred Thirty-Nine

For you gladly put up with fools, being wise yourselves! For you put up with it when someone makes slaves of you.
2 Cor 11.19-20

Comment
Fools!

***

One Hundred Forty

Agree with one another, live in peace.
2 Cor 13.11

Comment
Find agreement, share in kindness.

One Hundred Forty-One

There is no longer Jew or Greek, there is no longer slave or free, there is no longer male and female.
Gal 3.28

Comment
Be equal in freedom.

***

One Hundred Forty-Two

The elemental spirits of the world.
Gal 4.3 & Col 2.8

Comment
Delphi.

One Hundred Forty-Three

What the flesh desires is opposed to the Spirit, and what the Spirit desires is opposed to the flesh.
Gal 5.17

Comment
True and untrue.

***

One Hundred Forty-Four

Bear one another's burdens.
Gal 6.2

Comment
Shoulder the future.

One Hundred Forty-Five

Above every name that is named, not only in this age but also in the age to come.
Eph 1.21

Comment
Can this name be spoken?

***

One Hundred Forty-Six

Following the desires of flesh and senses, we were by nature children of wrath.
Eph 2.3

Comment
Reborn in love.

One Hundred Forty-Seven

We are what he has made us.
Eph 2.10

Comment
Think on these seven words.

∗∗∗

One Hundred Forty-Eight

Being rooted and grounded in love.
Eph 3.17

Comment
Seek God.

One Hundred Forty-Nine

Do not let the sun go down on your anger.
Eph 4.26

Comment
Make peace.

***

One Hundred Fifty

Let no evil talk come out of your mouths.
Eph 4.29

Comment
Kindness only.

One Hundred Fifty-One

Be kind to one another, tender-hearted, forgiving one another.
Eph 4.32

Comment
Interfaith and inter-relation, mosque, temple, shrine, church – New Pacific.

***

One Hundred Fifty-Two

A fragrant offering and sacrifice to God.
Eph 5.2

Comment
Your kindness shines brightest.

One Hundred Fifty-Three

Live as children of light.
Eph 5.8

Comment
All that's good and right and true.

***

One Hundred Fifty-Four

Wives, be subject to your husbands!
Eph 5.22 & Col. 3.18

Comment
Women must be subject to men?

One Hundred Fifty-Five

Slaves, obey your earthly masters with fear and trembling.
Eph 6.5

Comment
Why did he say this? Was that Paul?

***

One Hundred Fifty-Six

Put on the whole armor of God.
Eph 6.11

Comment
Against the cosmic powers of this present darkness.

One Hundred Fifty-Seven

Withstand on that evil day.
Eph 6.13

Comment
Stand firm!

***

One Hundred Fifty-Eight

Pray in the Spirit at all times in every prayer and supplication. To that end keep alert and always persevere in supplication for all.
Eph 6.18

Comment
Pray to love all life on earth.

One Hundred Fifty-Nine

And this is my prayer, that your love may overflow more and more with knowledge and full insight to help you to determine what is best.
Phil 1.9

Comment
Pray for this.

***

One Hundred Sixty

Be blameless and innocent children of God.
Phil 2.15

Comment
Shine like stars in the world.

One Hundred Sixty-One

I ask you also, my loyal companion, help these women, for they have struggled beside me in the work of the gospel.
Phil 4.3

Comment
Let women lead the world.

***

One Hundred Sixty-Two

Let your gentleness be known to everyone.
Phil 4.5

Comment
Think with love.

One Hundred Sixty-Three

If there is any excellence and there is anything worthy of praise, think about these things.
Phil 4.8

Comment
Find it and praise it.

***

One Hundred Sixty-Four

The mystery that has been hidden throughout the ages.
Col 1.26

Comment
Still hidden, still revealed.

One Hundred Sixty-Five

Forgive each other.
Col 3.13

Comment
Make yourself easy to forgive.

***

One Hundred Sixty-Six

Above all, clothe yourselves with love, which binds everything together in perfect harmony.
Col 3.14

Comment
Be active in love.

One Hundred Sixty-Seven

Devote yourselves to prayer, keeping alert in it with thanksgiving.
Col 4.2

Comment
Be resolute in prayer.

***

One Hundred Sixty-Eight

Pray for us as well that God will open to us a door for the word.
Col 4.3

Comment
Speak about love for God.

One Hundred Sixty-Nine

Let your speech always be gracious, seasoned with salt.
Col 4.6

Comment
Wise in gentleness.

***

One Hundred Seventy

To serve a living and true God.
1 Thess 1.9

Comment
Find this truth.

One Hundred Seventy-One

Not to please mortals.
1 Thess 2.4

Comment
To please God.

***

One Hundred Seventy-Two

Satan blocked our way.
1 Thess 2.18

Comment
Our way is love.

One Hundred Seventy-Three

For God did not call us to impurity.
1 Thess 4.7

Comment
Purity in kindness.

***

One Hundred Seventy-Four

Children of the day.
1 Thess 5.5

Comment
We are the sunlight.

One Hundred Seventy-Five

Rejoice always, pray without ceasing, give thanks in all circumstances.
1 Thess 5.16-18

Comment
We can be heaven.

***

One Hundred Seventy-Six

Hold fast to what is good.
1 Thess 5.21

Comment
Hold my hand.

One Hundred Seventy-Seven

Comfort your hearts and strengthen them in every good work and word.
2 Thess 2.17

Comment
Speak words of love.

***

One Hundred Seventy-Eight

With toil and labor we worked night and day.
2 Thess 3.8

Comment
Prayer unceasing.

One Hundred Seventy-Nine

Brothers and sisters, do not be weary in doing what is right.
2 Thess 3.13

Comment
Stand up for a better world.

***

One Hundred Eighty

Peace at all times in all ways.
2 Thess 3.16

Comment
Peace in all prisons.

One Hundred Eighty-One

Love that comes from a pure heart.
1 Tim 1.5

Comment
Learn me this.

***

One Hundred Eighty-Two

Show yourself in all respects a model of good works, and in your teaching show integrity, gravity, and sound speech that cannot be censured.
1 Titus 2.7

Comment
Be like a rainbow.

One Hundred Eighty-Three

Women should dress themselves modestly and decently in suitable clothing.
1 Tim 2.9

Comment
Same standards for all.

***

One Hundred Eighty-Four

I permit no woman to teach or to have authority over a man; she is to keep silent.
1 Tim 2.12

Comment
Disobey what is wrong.

One Hundred Eighty-Five

For everything created by God is good, and nothing is to be rejected, provided it is received with thanksgiving.
1 Tim 4.4

Comment
Reject the ignorance of man.

***

One Hundred Eighty-Six

Reading of scripture.
1 Tim 4.13

Comment
Read and share, bridge of faith.

One Hundred Eighty-Seven

Do not speak harshly to an older man, but speak to him as to a father, to younger men as brothers, to older women as mothers, to younger women as sisters – with absolute purity.
1 Tim 5.1-2

Comment
All are family.

***

One Hundred Eighty-Eight

Good works are conspicuous.
1 Tim 5.25

Comment
In a faithless world be conspicuous.

One Hundred Eighty-Nine

Love of money is a root of all kinds of evil.
1 Tim 6.10

Comment
Let money serve the cause of love.

***

One Hundred Ninety

Take hold of the eternal life.
1 Tim 6.12

Comment
Seize the light.

One Hundred Ninety-One

May the Lord grant mercy to the household of Onesiphorus, because he often refreshed me and was not ashamed of my chain.
2 Tim 1.16

Comment
Paul in prison c. 65 CE. Mercy for prisoners!

***

One Hundred Ninety-Two

The word of God is not chained.
2 Tim 2.9

Comment
It speaks in all.

One Hundred Ninety-Three

Not be quarrelsome but kindly to everyone.
2 Tim 2.24

Comment
Seek goodness in others.

***

One Hundred Ninety-Four

What persecutions I endured!
2 Tim 3.11

Comment
No more! Hands together in love.

One Hundred Ninety-Five

The time of my departure has come. I have fought the good fight, I have finished the race, I have kept the faith.
2 Tim 4.6-7

Comment
Courageous Paulos!

***

One Hundred Ninety-Six

To the pure all things are pure.
Titus 1.15

Comment
Action for love makes pure.

One Hundred Ninety-Seven

To the corrupt and unbelieving nothing is pure.
Titus 1.15

Comment
Corrupt no more!

***

One Hundred Ninety-Eight

The saying is sure.
Titus 3.8

Comment
Build bridges of love.

One Hundred Ninety-Nine

I have indeed received much joy and encouragement from your love.
Philemon 7

Comment
My brothers and sisters of all faiths, thank you.

***

Two Hundred

Do not worry about anything, but in everything by prayer and supplication with thanksgiving let your requests be made known to God.
Phil 4.6-7

Comment
The peace of God, which passeth all understanding, keep your hearts and minds in the knowledge and love of God – Saint Paul's blessing (BCP 1559).

Stean Anthony

I'm an Anglican Christian, based in Japan. I've written a series of books promoting understanding and peace between churches and different faiths. You can find out more about me in the MTMM series (*Messages to My Mother 1-7*), *One Hundred Poems*, *Inorijuzu*, *Mozzicone*, *Selections from Shakespeare I – IV*, *Songs 365*, published by Yamaguchi Shoten, Kyoto (2007-9). Also *Eco-Friendly Japan*, published by Eihosha, Tokyo (2008). Thanks to Yamaguchi H.T. for her kind help.

Afterword

All quotations from the New Revised Standard Version NRSV *Holy Bible* (New York: OUP, 1989). Japanese translation from Shinkyōdō translation, Japan Bible Society. 利用された翻訳は新共同訳（2002 年 5 月）日本聖書協会に参考下さい。<http://www.bible.or.jp/index.html>

I urge you to go back to the original and think upon it. I humbly beg the forgiveness of Saint Paul of Tarsus for the liberties I have taken in this book.

Author's profits from this publication to be donated to Oxfam Japan, with a request that it be used to build schools and improve educational facilities for children in Africa.

For change

www.oxfam.jp

Words of Prayer

I

How beautiful upon the mountains
Are the feet of the messenger
Who announces peace,
Who brings good news,
Who announces salvation.
Isaiah 52.7

II

O Lord, what are human beings
That you regard them,
Or mortals that you think of them?
They are like a breath,
Their days are like a passing shadow.
Psalm 144.3-4

III

If you remove the yoke from among you,
The pointing of the finger, the speaking of evil,
If you offer your food to the hungry
And satisfy the needs of the afflicted,
Then your light shall rise in the darkness
And your gloom be like the noonday.
Isaiah 58.9-10

IV

For you shall go out in joy,
And be led back in peace.
The mountains and the hills before you
Shall burst into song,
And all the trees of the field
Shall clap their hands.
Isaiah 55.12

V

Let the words of my mouth
And the meditation of my heart
Be acceptable to you,
O Lord, my rock and my redeemer,

                              Amen.

Psalm 19.14

Word of Blessing

A blessing of peace
Be with us
And between us
In the spirit of love
People of every faith.

In all things
Thanks be to God
Amen.

日本語の訳

1. 希望をもって喜び、苦難を耐え忍び、たゆまず祈りなさい。
   Rom 12.12
   Comment 祈るときに神に言い尽くすこと。
2. 兄弟愛をもって互いに愛し。 Rom 12.10
   Comment 壊れている世界を癒されよ。
3. それから、ひざまずいて、「主よ、この罪を彼らに負わせないでください」と大声で叫んだ。ステファノはこう言って、眠りについた。サウロは、ステファノの殺害に賛成していた。 Acts 7.60 – 8.1
   Comment サウロはパウロ。
4. その日、エルサレムの教会に対して大迫害が起こった。 Acts 8.1
   Comment 何とか生き抜け！
5. 一方、サウロは家から家へと押し入って教会を荒らし、男女を問わず引き出して牢に送っていた。 Acts 8.3
   Comment 自分を牢に閉じ込めてしまう。
6. ところが、サウロが旅をしてダマスコに近づいたとき、突然、天からの光が彼の周りを照らした。サウロは地に倒れ、「サウロ、サウロ、なぜ、わたしを迫害するのか」と呼びかける声を聞いた。「主よ、あなたはどなたですか」と言うと、答えがあった。「わたしは、あなたが迫害しているイエスである。」 Acts 9.3-5
   Comment サウロは三日間、目が見えず、食べも飲みもしなかった、35年ごろ。
7. 旅を続けてダマスコに近づいたときのこと、真昼ごろ、突然、天から強い光がわたしの周りを照らしました。 Acts 22.6
   Comment もっと愛しなさい。
8. 同行していた人たちは、声は聞こえても、だれの姿も見えな

いので、ものも言えず立っていた。 Acts 9.7
   Comment　やらねばならないことがわかる。
9. 主よ、どうしたらよいでしょうか。 Acts 22.10
   Comment　この言葉－自由を与えよ！
10. 今、何をためらっているのです。 Acts 22.16
    Comment　愛を実行！
11. すると、たちまち目からうろこのようなものが落ち、サウロは元どおり見えるようになった。 Acts 9.18
    Comment　嬉悲涙。
12. 行け。わたしがあなたを遠くに遣わすのだ。 Acts 22.21
    Comment　今日は女性をお召しに。
13. それから、バルナバはサウロを捜しにタルソスへ行き、見つけ出してアンティオキアに連れ帰った。 Acts 11.25-6
    Comment　古い壁、新しい祈り。
14. パウロとも呼ばれていたサウロは、聖霊に満たされ、魔術師をにらみつけて。 Acts 13.9
    Comment　愛を築け。
15. 兄弟たち、アブラハムの子孫の方々、ならびにあなたがたの中にいて神を畏れる人たち、この救いの言葉はわたしたちに送られました。 Acts 13.26
    Comment　もっと互いに愛し合い、平和の祈りで、それが理解されるように。
16. パウロは彼を見つめ、いやされるのにふさわしい信仰があるのを認め、「自分の足でまっすぐに立ちなさい」と大声で言った。すると、その人は躍り上がって歩きだした。 Acts 14.9-10
    Comment　他人を癒し、自分が癒される。
17. あるいは、何とかして人の気に入ろうとあくせくしているのでしょうか。 Gal 1.10
    Comment　人を喜ばせ、人を反省させ。

18. わたしにとっては、あなたがたから裁かれようと、人間の法廷で裁かれようと、少しも問題ではありません。わたしは、自分で自分を裁くことすらしません。 1 Cor 4.3
    Comment　　パウロのように自信たっぷり。
19. あなたがたが望むのはどちらですか。わたしがあなたがたのところへ鞭を持って行くことですか。 1 Cor 4.21
    Comment　　もっと哀れんでください。
20. ダマスコでアレタ王の代官が、わたしを捕えようとして、ダマスコの人たちの町を見張っていたとき、わたしは、窓から籠で城壁づたいにつり降ろされて、彼の手を逃れたのでした。 2 Cor 11.32-3
    Comment　　神を愛している人に自由を！
21. わたしは、キリストに結ばれていた一人の人を知っていますが、その人は十四年前、第三の天にまで引き上げられたのです。体のままか、体を離れてかは知りません。神がご存じです。わたしはそのような人を知っています。彼は楽園にまで引き上げられ、人が口にするのを許されない、言い表しえない言葉を耳にしたのです。 2 Cor 12.2-4
    Comment　　これはパウロだった。
22. それで、そのために思い上がることのないようにと、わたしの身に一つのとげが与えられました。 2 Cor 12.7
    Comment　　弱き、強きだ。
23. わたしパウロが、自分の手で挨拶を記します。 2 Thess 3.17
    Comment　　私の顔に見覚えないか。
24. すべての人に対してすべてのものになりました。何とかして何人かでも救うためです。 1 Cor 9.22
    Comment　　事情が変わっても、愛は変わらない。
25. わたしにふりかかったような迫害と苦難をもいといませんでした。そのような迫害にわたしは耐えました。 2 Tim 3.11

Comment　牢に閉じ込まれ、鞭打たれ、軽蔑され。
26. 安息日に町の門を出て、祈りの場所があると思われる川岸に行った。そして、わたしたちもそこに座って、集まっていた婦人たちに話をした。ティアティラ市出身の紫布を商う人で、神をあがめるリディアという婦人も話を聞いていたが、主が彼女の心を開かれたので、彼女はパウロの話を注意深く聞いた。 Acts 16.13-14

Comment　パウロの言葉を熱烈に理解するため、神様が彼女の心を開いた。

27. わたしたちは、祈りの場所に行く途中、占いの霊に取りつかれている女奴隷に出会った。この女は、占いをして主人たちに多くの利益を得させていた。彼女は、パウロやわたしたちの後ろについて来てこう叫ぶのであった。 Acts 16.16-17

Comment　「この人たちは、いと高き神の僕で、皆さんに救いの道を宣べ伝えているのです。」

28. 高官たちは、ローマ帝国の市民権を持つわたしたちを、裁判にもかけずに公衆の面前で鞭打ってから投獄したのに、今ひそかに釈放しようとするのか。いや、それはいけない。高官たちが自分でここへ来て、わたしたちを連れ出すべきだ。 Acts 16.37

Comment　不公平許さん。

29. 世界中を騒がせてきた連中が、ここにも来ています。 Acts 17.6

Comment　権威のものを倒せ、苦悩したものを救おう！

30. 道を歩きながら、あなたがたが拝むいろいろなものを見ていると、『知られざる神に』と刻まれている祭壇さえ見つけたからです。それで、あなたがたが知らずに拝んでいるもの、それをわたしはお知らせしましょう。 Acts 17.23

Comment　パウロはアテネにて、アレオパゴス。

31. 皆さんのうちのある詩人たちも、/『我らは神の中に生き、動き、存在する』/『我らもその子孫である』と、/言っているとおりです。 Acts 17.28
    Comment　古代ギリシャの詩人を引用。
32. 命がけでわたしの命を守ってくれたこの人たち。 Rom 16.4
    Comment　プリスカとアキラによろしく。 Acts 18.2. 1 Cor 16.19.
33. エフェソ人のアルテミスは偉い方！ Acts 19.28
    Comment　ディアナの神殿、世界の七不思議のひとつ。
34. 受けるよりは与える方が幸いである。 Acts 20.35
    Comment　哀れみ深いものは聖なるもの。
35. このように話してから、パウロは皆と一緒にひざまずいて祈った。人々は皆激しく泣き、パウロの首を抱いて接吻した。特に、自分の顔をもう二度と見ることはあるまいとパウロが言ったので、非常に悲しんだ。人々はパウロを船まで見送りに行った。 Acts 20.36-38
    Comment　パウロを愛していた。
36. パウロは言った。「わたしは確かにユダヤ人です。キリキア州のれっきとした町、タルソスの市民です。」 Acts 21.39
    Comment　わたしの友人に自由を与えてください！
37. この人には何の悪い点も見いだせない。霊か天使かが彼に話しかけたのだろうか。 Acts 23.9
    Comment　非難することに急ぐな。
38. その夜、主はパウロのそばに立って言われた。「勇気を出せ。」 Acts 23.11
    Comment　すべての囚人に手助けを。
39. 彼らの目を開いて、闇から光に。 Acts 26.18
    Comment　神に仕えることに召された。
40. こう言ってパウロは、一同の前でパンを取って神に感謝の祈りをささげてから、それを裂いて食べ始めた。 Acts 27.35

Comment　全員が無事に上陸した。
41. パウロはその家に行って祈り、手を置いていやした。 Acts 28.8
Comment　皆癒され。
42. あなたの考えておられることを、直接お聞きしたい。この分派については、至るところで反対があることを耳にしているのです。 Acts 28.22
Comment　真実の証拠。
43. あなたがたにぜひ会いたいのは、"霊"の賜物をいくらかでも分け与えて、力になりたいからです。あなたがたのところで、あなたがたとわたしが互いに持っている信仰によって、励まし合いたいのです。 Rom 1.11-12
Comment　信仰のバリアを飛び越え！
44. 「正しい者は信仰によって生きる」と書いてある。 Rom 1.17
Comment　古代の本を読め。
45. 真理ではなく不義に従う者には、怒りと憤りをお示しになります。 Rom 2.8
Comment　忍耐強く善を行い、栄光と誉れと不滅のものを求める者には、永遠の命をお与えになり。
46. 神はユダヤ人だけの神でしょうか。 Rom 3.29
Comment　時を越える神。
47. 聖書には何と書いてありますか。「アブラハムは神を信じた。それが、彼の義と認められた」とあります。 Rom 4.3
Comment　上、上に持ち上げる強い信仰。
48. 苦難は忍耐を、忍耐は練達を、練達は希望を生むということ。 Rom 5.3-4
Comment　ほかの存在の苦労を減らす！
49. 罪が支払う報酬は死です。 Rom 6.23
Comment　罪とは何だろうか。
50. 霊に従う新しい生き方。 Rom 7.6

Comment　もっと愛し、他は捨て。
51. わたしは自分の望む善は行わず。 Rom 7.19
Comment　エルサレムに平和たて。
52. もし神がわたしたちの味方であるならば、だれがわたしたちに敵対できますか。 Rom 8.31
Comment　魂、善良を照らし！
53. 造られた物が造った者に、「どうしてわたしをこのように造ったのか」と言えるでしょうか。 Rom 9.20
Comment　不完全に生まれる。
54. 「良い知らせを伝える者の足は、なんと美しいことか」と書いてあるとおりです。 Rom 10.15
Comment　彼は平和を告げ、恵みの良い知らせを伝え／救いを告げ／あなたの神は王となられた。 Isaiah 52.7.
55. 実に、信仰は聞くことによって始まるのです。 Rom 10.17
Comment　天国に開け。
56. 野生のオリーブであるあなたが、その代わりに接ぎ木され。 Rom 11.17
Comment　愛し合うように互いに奉仕する。
57. ああ、神の富と知恵と知識のなんと深いことか。Rom 11.33
Comment　歌え！
58. 愛には偽りがあってはなりません。悪を憎み、善から離れず。 Rom 12.9
Comment　隣人の間に納得。
59. 聖なる者たちの貧しさを自分のものとして彼らを助け、旅人をもてなすよう努めなさい。 Rom 12.13

Comment 聖人と旅人から学ぶ。
60. あなたがたを迫害する者のために祝福を祈りなさい。祝福を祈るのであって、呪ってはなりません。 Rom 12.14
Comment 常に善良心でこたえ。
61. 互いに思いを一つにし。 Rom 12.16
Comment 地上すべての存在に調和。
62. 身分の低い人々と交わりなさい。 Rom 12.16
Comment もっと幸福な人生を与えよう。
63. 愛する人たち、自分で復讐せず。 Rom 12.19
Comment 愛してあげる。
64. あなたの敵が飢えていたら食べさせ、渇いていたら飲ませよ。 Rom 12.20
Comment 友にする。
65. 人は皆、上に立つ権威に従うべきです。神に由来しない権威はなく、今ある権威はすべて神によって立てられたものだからです。 Rom 13.1
Comment このシーザーは違う！地下に潜る。
66. 隣人を自分のように愛しなさい。 Rom 13.9
Comment みなは隣人。
67. 愛は隣人に悪を行いません。だから、愛は律法を全うするものです。 Rom 13.10
Comment 優しい心で互いに愛し合いなさい。
68. あなたがたが眠りから覚めるべき時が既に来ています。 Rom 13.11
Comment 明け方に。

69. 夜は更け、日は近づいた。 Rom 13.12
    Comment 希望が湧く。
70. 光の武具を身に着けましょう。 Rom 13.12
    Comment 神は愛。
71. ある日を他の日よりも尊ぶ人もいれば、すべての日を同じように考える人もいます。 Rom 14.5
    Comment この日は聖日。
72. ケンクレアイの教会の奉仕者でもある、わたしたちの姉妹フェベを紹介します。 Rom 16.1
    Comment 使徒のように歓迎。
73. 神は真実な方です。 1 Cor 1.9
    Comment パウロはこの言葉を好んだ。
74. 皆、勝手なことを言わず、仲違いせず、心を一つにし、思いを一つにして、固く結び合いなさい。 1 Cor 1.10
    Comment 未来をつかむために。
75. 神は世の知恵を愚かなものにされたではないか。 1 Cor 1.20
    Comment 誠の愛は愚かなもの。
76. ところが、神は、力ある者に恥をかかせるため、世の無力な者を選ばれました。 1 Cor 1.27
    Comment 強き、弱き。
77. 目が見もせず、耳が聞きもせず、人の心に思い浮かびもしなかったこと。 1 Cor 2.9
    Comment 卓越した栄光の隠された真実。
78. 霊的なものによって霊的なことを説明するのです。 1 Cor

2.13
Comment 魂を吹き通す風。
79. お互いの間にねたみや争いが絶えない以上、あなたがたは肉の人であり。 1 Cor 3.3
Comment 霊に結ばれている人たちは親切な心で出会う。
80. 神の神殿は聖なるものだからです。あなたがたはその神殿なのです。 1 Cor 3.17
Comment 地上全生命。
81. 先走って何も裁いてはいけません。 1 Cor 4.5
Comment 害が行えないため、善良を言う。
82. 侮辱されては祝福し、迫害されては耐え忍び、ののしられては優しい言葉を返しています。 1 Cor 4.12-13
Comment これがいい。
83. 世の屑。 1 Cor 4.13
Comment 至る所にゴミを拾う。
84. 愛と柔和な心で。 1 Cor 4.21
Comment 地球の掃除をする。
85. 洗われ、聖なる者とされ。 1 Cor 6.11
Comment 憎しみは愛に変わった。
86. この世の有様は過ぎ去るからです。 1 Cor 7.31
Comment この世は常に最後に向かっている。
87. では、わたしの報酬とは何でしょうか。 1 Cor 9.18
Comment 愛されて、愛する。
88. あなたがたは知らないのですか。競技場で走る者は皆走る

けれども、賞を受けるのは一人だけです。 1 Cor 9.24
Comment　皆は賞を受ける。

89. あなたがたも賞を得るように走りなさい。 1 Cor 9.24
Comment　一番を勝ち取れ。

90. すべてに節制します。 1 Cor 9.25
Comment　他の存在に苦労を与えない。

91. 神は真実な方です。あなたがたを耐えられないような試練に遭わせることはなさらず、試練と共に、それに耐えられるよう、逃れる道をも備えていてくださいます。 1 Cor 10.13
Comment　愛が家に入るように、開門

92. 偶像礼拝を避けなさい。 1 Cor 10.14
Comment　憎しみと怒り、これは偶像

93. パンは一つだから、わたしたちは大勢でも一つの体です。皆が一つのパンを分けて食べるからです。 1 Cor 10.17
Comment　一緒に平和のパンを裂く。

94. ふさわしいかどうか、自分で判断しなさい。 1 Cor 11.13
Comment　女が頭に何もかぶらないで神に祈るのか。

95. わたしの記念としてこのように行いなさい。 1 Cor 11.24-25
Comment　あなたはわたしに愛されていると覚えて。

96. いろいろあります。 1 Cor 12.4-6
Comment　愛以外はリアルはない。

97. ある人には"霊"によって知恵の言葉、ある人には同じ"霊"によって知識の言葉が与えられ、ある人にはその同じ"霊"によって信仰、ある人にはこの唯一の"霊"によって病気をいやす力。 1 Cor 12.8-10

Comment　それぞれの人、それぞれの才能。
98. 多くの部分があっても、一つの体なのです。　1 Cor 12.20
Comment　また我々を一つにまとめ。
99. たとえ、人々の異言、天使たちの異言を語ろうとも、愛がなければ、わたしは騒がしいどら、やかましいシンバル。1 Cor 13.1
Comment　諧調をなして鳴り響く、平和あれ。
100. たとえ、預言する賜物を持ち、あらゆる神秘とあらゆる知識に通じていようとも、たとえ、山を動かすほどの完全な信仰を持っていようとも、愛がなければ、無に等しい。1 Cor 13.2
Comment　この真実に神を見つける。
101. 全財産を貧しい人々のために使い尽くそうとも、誇ろうとしてわが身を死に引き渡そうとも、愛がなければ、わたしに何の益もない。1 Cor 13.3（この節には異文がある）
Comment　感謝の心をどのように表したらいい。
102. たといまた、わたしが自分の全財産を人に施しても、また、自分のからだを焼かれるために渡しても、もし愛がなければ、いっさいは無益である。(口語訳) 1 Cor. 13.3
Comment　友のために自分の命を捨てること、これ以上に大きな愛はない。
103. 愛は忍耐強い。愛は情け深い。1 Cor 13.4
Comment　愛についていて。
104. 愛はすべてを忍び、すべてを信じ、すべてを望み、すべてに耐える。1 Cor 13.7

Comment　すでに我を超え、神秘的な明け渡し。
105. 愛は決して滅びない。 1 Cor 13.8
　　Comment　これを信じて。
106. わたしたちの知識は一部分。 1 Cor 13.9
　　Comment　いつか、すべて完全。
107. わたしたちは、今は、鏡におぼろに映ったものを見ている。だがそのときには、顔と顔とを合わせて見ることになる。
　　1 Cor 13.12
　　Comment　神の愛のエニグマ。
108. わたしは、今は一部しか知らなくとも、そのときには、はっきり知られているようにはっきり知ることになる。 1 Cor 13.12
　　Comment　今日全部はない、明日完璧。
109. それゆえ、信仰と、希望と、愛、この三つは、いつまでも残る。その中で最も大いなるものは、愛である。 1 Cor 13.13
　　Comment　もし教義が「愛をしない」と言えば、その教義を捨てなさい。
110. 愛を追い求めなさい。 1 Cor. 14.1
　　Comment　ギリシャ語アガペー、ラテン語カリタス、中国・韓国・日本・愛。互いに愛し合いなさい。
111. 笛であれ竪琴であれ。 1 Cor 14.7
　　Comment　心に響く美しい曲。
112. 婦人たちは、教会では黙っていなさい。 1 Cor 14.34
　　Comment　恐れるな。語り続けよ。黙っているな。わたしがあなたと共にいる。

113. そして最後に、月足らずで生まれたようなわたしにも現れました。わたしは、神の教会を迫害したのですから、使徒たちの中でもいちばん小さな者であり、使徒と呼ばれる値打ちのない者です。 1 Cor 15.8-9

　　Comment　パウロに与えられた神の恵みは無駄にならず。

114. わたしは他のすべての使徒よりずっと多く働きました。しかし、働いたのは、実はわたしではなく、わたしと共にある神の恵みなのです。 1 Cor 15.10

　　Comment　誇りとしているだろうか。

115. そちらに着いたら、あなたがたから承認された人たちに手紙を持たせて、その贈り物を届けにエルサレムに行かせましょう。 1 Cor 16.3

　　Comment　平和の賜物を交換 － すべての信仰。

116. 目を覚ましていなさい。信仰に基づいてしっかり立ちなさい。雄々しく強く生きなさい。何事も愛をもって行いなさい。 1 Cor 16.13-14

　　Comment　愛を妨げる垣根を破り倒せ！

117. 聖なる口づけによって互いに挨拶を交わしなさい。 1 Cor 16.20

　　Comment　手と手優しく触れ合う。

118. マラナ・タ あるいは マラン・アタ。 1 Cor 16.22

　　Comment　愛、心にて、もっと輝いて。

119. あなたがたの喜びのために協力する者です。 2 Cor 1.24

　　Comment　各自それぞれ、愛の目的。

120. 赦して、力づけるべき。 2 Cor 2.7

Comment　愛を再び肯定する。
121. 命から命に至らせる香り。 2 Cor 2.16
Comment　天のそよ風。
122. 霊は生かします。 2 Cor 3.6
Comment　霊、愛の真実を明かしてください。
123. 覆いは取り去られます。 2 Cor 3.16
Comment　燦然と輝く光の中の愛。
124.「闇から光が輝き出よ」と命じられた神は、わたしたちの心の内に輝いて。 2 Cor 4.6
Comment　聖なる油を燃やして点すランプ。
125. 宝を土の器に納めています。 2 Cor 4.7
Comment　心の中に神の言葉。
126. 四方から苦しめられても行き詰まらず。 2 Cor 4.8
Comment　必要に応じて、愛のために苦労。
127. たとえわたしたちの「外なる人」は衰えていくとしても、わたしたちの「内なる人」は日々新たにされていきます。 2 Cor 4.16
Comment　内面にもっと明るい魂。
128. わたしたちは見えるものではなく、見えないものに目を注ぎます。見えるものは過ぎ去りますが、見えないものは永遠に存続するからです 2 Cor 4.18
Comment　錯覚を越え、向こうに。
129. 古いものは過ぎ去り、新しいものが生じた。 2 Cor 5.17
Comment　毎日新しい。
130. わたしたちは人を欺いているようでいて、誠実であり、人

に知られていないようでいて、よく知られ。 2 Cor 6.8-9

    Comment　同じ真実、新しい装い。

131. 心を広くしてください。 2 Cor 6.13

    Comment　アフリカの上に虹がまたぐ。

132. わたしたちに心を開いてください。 2 Cor 7.2

    Comment　悲しみに生まれた子。

133. 惜しんでわずかしか種を蒔かない者は、刈り入れもわずかで、惜しまず豊かに蒔く人は、刈り入れも豊かなのです。 2 Cor 9.6

    Comment　活動的に善をなす。

134. 喜んで与える人を神は愛してくださる。 2 Cor 9.7

    Comment　毎日施し。

135. 彼は惜しみなく分け与え、貧しい人に施した。 2 Cor 9.9 & Ps 112.9

    Comment　アフリカを援助せよ！

136. わたしのことを、「手紙は重々しく力強いが、実際に会ってみると弱々しい人で、話もつまらない」と言う者たちがいるからです。 2 Cor 10.10

    Comment　パウロについて、パウロによって。逆が正しい？

137. わたしがあなたがたを愛していないからだろうか。神がご存じ！ 2 Cor 11.11

    Comment　その愛、わかるように知らせよ！

138. サタンでさえ光の天使を装うのです。 2 Cor 11.14

    Comment　嫌悪感と利己心はサタン。

139. 賢いあなたがたのことだから、喜んで愚か者たちを我慢し

てくれるでしょう。実際、あなたがたはだれかに奴隷にされても、我慢しています。 2 Cor 11.19-20

Comment　愚か者！

140. 思いを一つにしなさい。平和を保ちなさい。 2 Cor 13.11

Comment　愛と平和の神があなたがたと共に。

141. そこではもはや、ユダヤ人もギリシア人もなく、奴隷も自由な身分の者もなく、男も女もありません。 Gal 3.28

Comment　自由を持って、平等。

142. 世を支配する諸霊。 Gal 4.3 & Col 2.8

Comment　デルフィ。

143. 肉の望むところは、霊に反し、霊の望むところは、肉に反するからです。 Gal 5.17

Comment　正解か誤りか。

144. 互いに重荷を担いなさい。 Gal 6.2

Comment　未来を負う。

145. 今の世ばかりでなく、来るべき世にも唱えられるあらゆる名の上に置かれました。 Eph 1.21

Comment　この名は申されますか？

146. 肉や心の欲するままに行動していたのであり、ほかの人々と同じように、生まれながら神の怒りを受けるべき者でした。 Eph 2.3

Comment　愛によって生まれ変わった。

147. わたしたちは神に造られたものであり。 Eph 2.10

Comment　この七つの言葉に熟考。（英語を参照して下さい）

148. あなたがたを愛に根ざし、愛にしっかりと立つ者。
    Eph 3.17
    Comment　神を捜し求め。
149. 日が暮れるまで怒ったままでいてはいけません。
    Eph 4.26
    Comment　和解をする。
150. 悪い言葉を一切口にしてはなりません。 Eph 4.29
    Comment　優しい言葉だけ。
151. 互いに親切にし、憐れみの心で接し、赦し合いなさい。
    Eph 4.32
    Comment　インターフェイスと相互関係・モスク・寺・神社・教会・新太平洋。(インターフェイス―信仰を互いに認め合うこと、英語の interfaith と interface.)
152. 香りのよい供え物、つまりいけにえとして。 Eph 5.2
    Comment　親切心が最も輝く。
153. 光の子として歩みなさい。 Eph 5.8
    Comment　あらゆる善意と正義と真実。
154. 妻たちよ、自分の夫に仕えなさい。Eph 5.22 & Col. 3.18
    Comment　女は男に仕えないといけない？
155. 奴隷たち、恐れおののき、真心を込めて、肉による主人に従いなさい。 Eph 6.5
    Comment　なぜそんなことを言ったのだろう？それはパウロだったのだろうか？
156. 神の武具を身に着けなさい。 Eph 6.11
    Comment　支配と権威、暗闇の世界に対抗。

157. 邪悪な日によく抵抗。 Eph 6.13
    Comment　しっかりこらえて。
158. どのような時にも、"霊"に助けられて祈り、願い求め、すべての聖なる者たちのために、絶えず目を覚まして根気よく祈り続けなさい。 Eph 6.18
    Comment　すべての存在を愛するために祈れ。
159. わたしは、こう祈ります。知る力と見抜く力とを身に着けて、あなたがたの愛がますます豊かになり、本当に重要なことを見分けられるように。 Phil 1.9
    Comment　この助けが与えられるために祈れ。
160. とがめられるところのない清い者となり、非のうちどころのない神の子として。 Phil 2.15
    Comment　世にあって星のように輝き。
161. なお、真実の協力者よ、あなたにもお願いします。この二人の婦人を支えてあげてください。二人は、命の書に名を記されているクレメンスや他の協力者たちと力を合わせて、福音のためにわたしと共に戦ってくれたのです。 Phil 4.3
    Comment　女性に世界を指導する権利与え。
162. あなたがたの広い心がすべての人に知られるようになさい。 Phil 4.5
    Comment　愛によって思え。.
163. 徳や称賛に値することがあれば、それを心に留めなさい。 Phil 4.8
    Comment　それを見つけて、褒めたたえ。
164. 世の初めから代々にわたって隠されていた、秘められた。

Col 1.26

Comment　まだ隠されて、すでに明かしている。

165. 赦し合いなさい。 Col 3.13

Comment　許されやすいようにして。

166. 愛を身に着けなさい。愛は、すべてを完成させるきずなです。 Col 3.14

Comment　愛のための活躍増やせ！

167. 目を覚まして感謝を込め、ひたすら祈りなさい。 Col 4.2

Comment　祈りに頑固。

168. わたしたちのためにも祈ってください。神が御言葉のために門を開いて。 Col 4.3

Comment　神の愛について語れ。

169. いつも、塩で味付けされた快い言葉で語りなさい。 Col 4.6

Comment　親切で知恵深く。

170. 生けるまことの神に仕えるように。 1 Thess 1.9

Comment　この真実を発見。

171. 人に喜ばれるためではなく。 1 Thess 2.4

Comment　神に喜んでいただくため。

172. サタンによって妨げられました。 1 Thess 2.18

Comment　愛は私たちの道。

173. 神がわたしたちを招かれたのは、汚れた生き方ではなく。 1 Thess 4.7

Comment　親切で純粋なこころ。

174. 昼の子。 1 Thess 5.5

Comment　私たちは日光。
175. いつも喜んでいなさい。絶えず祈りなさい。どんなことにも感謝しなさい。 1 Thess 5.16-18
Comment　天国は私たちの内に生きられる。
176. 良いものを大事にしなさい。 1 Thess 5.21
Comment　私の手を握れ。
177. どうか、あなたがたの心を励まし、また強め、いつも善い働きをし、善い言葉を語る者としてくださるように。
2 Thess 2.17
Comment　愛の言葉をいい。
178. 夜昼大変苦労して、働き続けた。 2 Thess 3.8
Comment　絶えず祈れ！
179. そして、兄弟たち、あなたがたは、たゆまず善いことをしなさい。 2 Thess 3.13
Comment　公平な世界・バリアフリー世界を擁護！
180. いついかなる場合にも、あなたがたに平和。 2 Thess 3.16
Comment　牢にいる人に平和心。
181. 清い心と正しい良心と純真な信仰とから生じる愛。
1 Tim 1.5
Comment　これを学ばせ！
182. あなた自身、良い行いの模範となりなさい。教えるときには、清廉で品位を保ち、非難の余地のない健全な言葉を語りなさい。 Titus 2.6-7
Comment　虹になれ！
183. 婦人はつつましい身なりをし、慎みと貞淑をもって身を飾

るべきであり。 1 Tim 2.9

Comment　男女平等、同じ基準。

184. 婦人が教えたり、男の上に立ったりするのを、わたしは許しません。むしろ、静かにしているべきです。 1 Tim 2.12

Comment　思い切って言う－間違った指示に従うな！

185. 神がお造りになったものはすべて良いものであり、感謝して受けるならば、何一つ捨てるものはないからです。
1 Tim 4.4

Comment　男に受け入れられた無知を捨てる。

186. 聖書の朗読。 1 Tim 4.13

Comment　読んで、共にする、インターフェイスの架け橋。

187. 老人を叱ってはなりません。むしろ、自分の父親と思って諭しなさい。若い男は兄弟と思い、年老いた婦人は母親と思い、若い女性には常に清らかな心で姉妹と思って諭しなさい。 1 Tim 5.1-2

Comment　皆は家族だ。

188. 良い行いも明白。 1 Tim 5.25

Comment　この世にくっきり立つ。

189. 金銭の欲は、すべての悪の根です。 1 Tim 6.10

Comment　愛のために金。

190. 永遠の命を手に入れ。 1 Tim 6.12

Comment　光をつかんで。

191. どうか、主がオネシフォロの家族を憐れんでくださいますように。彼は、わたしをしばしば励まし、わたしが囚人の身であることを恥とも思わず。 2 Tim 1.16

Comment　パウロは65年ごろ刑務所にて。囚人に哀れみ！
192. わたしは苦しみを受け、ついに犯罪人のように鎖につながれています。しかし、神の言葉はつながれていません。 2 Tim 2.9

Comment　すべてに開かれている。
193. 争わず、すべての人に柔和に。 2 Tim 2.24

Comment　他人の良い心を捜し求め。
194. 迫害にわたしは耐えました。 2 Tim 3.11

Comment　迫害から抜け出して。愛のために手と手を。
195. 世を去る時が近づきました。わたしは、戦いを立派に戦い抜き、決められた道を走りとおし、信仰を守り抜きました。 2 Tim 4.6-7

Comment　勇ましいパウロス。
196. 清い人には、すべてが清いのです。 Titus 1.15

Comment　愛の活動は清める。
197. 汚れている者、信じない者には、何一つ清いものはなく。 Titus 1.15

Comment　汚れなし！
198. この言葉は真実です。 Titus 3.8

Comment　愛の橋を架けるが良い。
199. わたしはあなたの愛から大きな喜びと慰めを得ました。 Philemon 7

Comment　シスターとブラザー、全信仰の兄弟姉妹に感謝。
200. どんなことでも、思い煩うのはやめなさい。何事につけ、

感謝を込めて祈りと願いをささげ、求めているものを神に打ち明けなさい。 Phil 4.6-7

Comment **The peace of God, which passeth all understanding, keep your hearts and minds in the knowledge and love of God – Saint Paul's blessing (BCP 1559) based upon Phil 4.7**

Words of Prayer

I

いかに美しいことか
山々を行き巡り、
良い知らせを伝える者の足は。
彼は平和を告げ、
恵みの良い知らせを伝え
救いを告げ
あなたの神は王となられた、と
シオンに向かって呼ばわる。
Isaiah 52.7

II

主よ、人間とは何ものなのでしょう
あなたがこれに親しまれるとは。
人の子とは何ものなのでしょう
あなたが思いやってくださるとは。
人間は息にも似たもの
彼の日々は消え去る影。
Psalm 144.3-4

III

くびきを負わすこと、指をさすこと
呪いの言葉をはくことを
あなたの中から取り去るなら。
飢えている人に心を配り
苦しめられている人の願いを満たすなら
あなたの光は、闇の中に輝き出で
あなたを包む闇は、真昼のようになる。
Isaiah 58.9-10

IV

あなたたちは喜び祝いながら出で立ち
平和のうちに導かれて行く。
山と丘はあなたたちを迎え
歓声をあげて喜び歌い
野の木々も、手をたたく。
Isaiah 55.12

V

どうか、わたしの口の言葉が御旨にかない
心の思いが御前に置かれますように。
主よ、わたしの岩、わたしの贖い主よ。アーメン。
Psalm 19.15

祝福の言葉

	愛の真心で
平和の祝福	常に
われわれと共に	絶えず
われわれの間に	主なる神に感謝、
	アーメン。

MTMM series
SAINT PAUL 200 (聖パウロ 200語 日本語訳付)
Compiled by Stean Anthony

Company : Yamaguchi Shoten
Address : 72 Tsukuda-cho, Ichijoji
Sakyo-ku, Kyoto, 606-8175
Japan
Tel. 075-781-6121
Fax. 075-705-2003
URL : http://www.yamaguchi-shoten.co.jp
E-mail : yamakyoto-606@jade.dti.ne.jp

MTMM series
SAINT PAUL 200
(聖パウロ 200語 日本語訳付)　　定価 本体500円(税別)

2010年3月20日 初 版

編　者　Stean　Anthony
発行者　山 口 冠 弥
印刷所　大村印刷株式会社
発行所　株式会社　山口書店
〒606-8175京都市左京区一乗寺築田町72
TEL：075-781-6121　FAX：075-705-2003
出張所電話
　　　東京03-5690-0051　　　中部058-275-4024
　　　福岡092-713-8575

ISBN 978-4-8411-0893-4　C1182
©2010 Stean Anthony